IN THE SHADOW OF
My Daughter's Death

PATRICIA VARNER

Copyright © 2022 by Patricia Varner

All rights reserved. No part of this publication may be reproduced, stored in a retrieval system, or transmitted, in any form, or by any means, electronic, mechanical, recorded, photocopied, or otherwise without the prior permission of the copyright owner, except by a reviewer who may quote brief passages in a review.

Printed in the United States of America

ISBN: 979-8-9870183-0-9

LCCN: 2022918017

Introduction

My name is Patricia, and I decided to write this book to tell you the story of my eldest daughter. Her name was Kemeil Patrice Thompson, and she died of cancer, but cancer is not the real story. Yes, it's a part of it, but it is not the main theme of this book.

In Psalms 23:4 (KJV) it says, "Yea, though I walk through the valley of the shadow of death, I will fear no evil."

Have you ever walked in the shadow of someone else's death?

I have -- my daughter's.

As I tell you my heart-breaking account of my daughter's ordeal with cancer, I also want to tell you of God's long-suffering, grace, and mercy.

I feel that bringing Kemeil's story from the background into the forefront can encourage someone who once knew Jesus Christ as their Lord and Savior but walked away to come back home before it's too late.

To write this book was painful. I revisited memories I'd rather not recount. No mother ever expects to bury a daughter and certainly not at her age. Recollections of the events that led to her death constantly pass through my mind. Sometimes those recollections trigger a flood of emotions. But I'm willing to share my anguish if it means that maybe someone will connect to her struggles and make an about face to return to Christ (or come to Christ for the first time).

"This is my story/this is my song/praising my Savior/all the day long." Welcome to our story.

My Prayer

Lord, let each word, each sentence, each paragraph be saturated in your presence. As the reader turns the pages, let the words and your Holy Spirit bring healing, encouragement, and hope to the wounded. In Jesus Name I pray, Amen.

Dedication

I dedicate this book to my family. We went through this process together.

To my mother who, from birth, had a special connection with Kemeil. In my mom's last days (she had dementia and Alzheimer's), she couldn't remember that Kemeil died. Those conversations were very hard, especially when she asked why Kemeil didn't come to see her. Mom didn't remember going to the funeral, either. On January 24, 2021, my mom passed away; in the same month, Kemeil died. I buried her in the same plot with Kemeil, and now they rest in peace together.

To my youngest daughter, Lisa Marie Coleman, and my son-in-law, Harold A. Coleman (best daughter and son-in-law in the world). Words cannot express my love and gratitude to them who, as a newlywed couple, took on the responsibilities they did for Kemeil.

To my brother, Mark Moultrie, and my sister-in-law, Cassandra Moultrie. Both stayed on the phone with me for untold hours, throughout many meltdowns, breakdowns, and mental crashes. I can never thank you both enough for your love and support even until this day.

To my many friends, co-workers, spiritual leaders, and all the precious saints of God. Without you all, this journey would have been a whole lot more painful. Thanks for your continued prayers, concerns, the visits to Kemeil (while she was sick) at home, in the nursing home, in the ICU, and in the hospitals. And yes, thanks also for lots and lots of laughs in the mist of all this

What I want you to know

I've saved the biggest, greatest accolades and honor for my Lord and Savior Jesus Christ. I wanted to give God a section by Himself. I want you to know that without God, there would be no book because there would be no me. I can now understand (not endorse or agree with) why those who can't handle stress on their own turn to ungodly things to try and take away the pain. I hate to think what would have become of me if I didn't have the Holy Ghost in me. It was God that gave me strength to walk those hospital hallways every day to go see my dying daughter. It was God who helped me to get out of bed when I just wanted to stay there all day in a ball. It was God who gave me scriptures for strength, dreams, and even words to say to Kemeil when I didn't know what else to say.

I don't know how people make it through these stressful times without the Lord. Thank you, Jesus, for everything!

Table of Contents

Chapter One: How Kemeil Came to Be 1

Chapter Two: In The Absence of Fathers 5

Chapter Three: When Cancer Arrived 9

Chapter Four: Without Peace 13

Chapter Five: From Bad, To Worse, To God in PA 20

Chapter Six: Released 26

Chapter Seven: God So Loved Kemeil 34

Chapter Eight: Silver Springs 43

Chapter Nine: The Last Day 49

Chapter Ten: The Book of Whys 55

Gone But not forgotten 61

Poetry from the heart of Kemeil Patrice Thompson 61

The Night I Understood My Mother 63

A Cause To Relax 64

A Doorkeeper's Prayer 66

Forgetting Something? 67

A Faithful Relationship 69

The Testimony 71

Look Up 73
Grandpa 75
Thinking Out Loud 78
The Responsibility 81
It's Alright 82

Good Times... 84

CHAPTER ONE
How Kemeil Came to Be

Kemeil Patrice Thompson was born on December 28, 1979. She died January 11, 2018 at 38 years old of metastatic adenocarcinoma of unknown primary. The cancer appeared first in the abdomen, went to her lungs, and then it spread to her brain where she developed five tumors. Right before she died, the cancer had also spread to her pelvis.

Kemeil was smart, beautiful, talented, and humorous. But, on the inside, she was always a troubled young lady. It started in her childhood, and it grew to its worst in adulthood. Being a young, single mother, I missed a lot of the warning signs of her mental struggles. I became pregnant with her at sixteen and gave birth to her at seventeen. I didn't fully know how to take care of myself, so I definitely didn't know how to care for a "surprise baby."

At sixteen, I was very naïve, and I didn't have confidence in my looks. When Kemeil's father, who was twenty-three-years-old, paid me some attention, I was an easy target. When we got involved, he told me I didn't need to worry about getting pregnant because he couldn't have children. Yes, I fell for that lie! I felt like the last person on earth who got tricked that way. To add insult to injury, I later found out that the guy had other children before he ever met me.

So, after this total disruption in my young life, I didn't know what to do. I remember "how" I found out I was pregnant. I got up like any other day to go to high school, but instead, I ran to the bathroom to throw up. I thought I had a stomach virus and just went on my way. But then, it happened the next day and the next. My older sister, Hermena, knew right away what was going on and she told me. I was horrified; my church-going mother was going to kill me. So, I went to the doctor (my childhood doctor, by the way, to add more shame to my situation) and behold…my mother showed up just when the doctor was about to give me my blood test results!

"Lord, have mercy," I thought, "I'm going to be killed at the doctor's office!"

Of course, you've already figured out, my test was positive. Stupid rabbit should have lived! (In case you don't know what I just said, that just used to be a term we used for a positive pregnancy test. Google search the Rabbit Test.)

My mother didn't say one word. I guess there were too many witnesses around, so she would kill me at home. That was the longest walk of my life. I had to face the crazy woman that just happened to be my mother. So, home I went, and we argued. My church-going mother (to my shock) told me to have an abortion. I had been to her church long enough to know that they didn't believe in abortions! So, I did what any sixteen-year-old did when they "just got caught big time." Whatever my mother told me to do, I said I was going to do the opposite.

"I'm keeping this baby," I said.

You can kind of figure out how the rest of the conversation went.

Well, the drama continued. My mother went to church; I don't know what happened there but, when she came home, she told me I was going to keep the baby! What? Oh no she didn't!

"No, I'm not keeping this baby," I replied.

That's right folks, Kemeil was supposed to be aborted.

In 1979, we still had telephone booths not cell phones. I went outside to a pay phone and called a hospital to arrange an abortion. Thank God I was underage. The hospital said I needed parental consent. I went home angry that my mother won this argument, and I ate crow for dinner.

Looking back at it all, I wish I could have changed many things. Back then, it wasn't like it is now. Getting pregnant outside of marriage was something people looked down upon. I might as well have been wearing a scarlet letter "A" on my chest like in the book. Instead of "A" for adulterer, mine would have been "F" for fornicator.

Facing my mother, neighbors, friends, and even enemies every day was difficult. I would have been a senior the next school year, but that was down the drain. Thank God I did have people who helped me. The school counselors said I would have enough credits to graduate if I took an advanced class in English during that summer. I thank God for his mercy and favor that I didn't have to go through my twelfth grade year in high school while pregnant.

Thus far, I hope this has given you some perspective on how unprepared I was for motherhood. Even after Kemeil was born, I still had emotional issues dealing with being a mother. I really hope that, if you are having sex outside of marriage, you will think hard about what you're doing. I had emotional scars from my experiences, and I passed some of those issues onto my daughter. Though I didn't mean to and I didn't know that's what I was doing, I did so anyway.

My mother continued to pray for me and petition God to bring me into the church and save my soul. She asked her church family to pray for me as well. Because of all those prayers going up for me, God fixed it. One day, her pastor, Bishop H.L. Brown of Progressive Holiness Church Inc., reached out and invited me to a revival service. I was a lot of things in my youth, but disrespectful to adults was generally not one of them. My mother had taught me better. That respect, coupled with the fear of dying that God put in my heart if I did not go, is why I started going to church.

Once I was introduced to a need for my soul to be saved, I got on the altar and prayed to God to save my soul. I had a lot of things I had to let go of and give up. My biggest battle was believing that God would fill a sinner like me with the Holy Ghost. Despite all my sins and failures, God saved me on January 20, 1983.

CHAPTER TWO
In The Absence of Fathers

Before the Lord saved me, I had some cleaning up to do. Kemeil's father wasn't a good person, so I had to let him go. Thank God we had never married. Kemeil never got to know him, and this is something I later regretted. At the time, I thought it was best to keep my distance from him which included keeping him away from his daughter. I didn't know until Kemeil was a young adult that she wanted to at least meet him. While growing up, she didn't ask me a lot of questions about him, so I didn't know that meeting him was important to her. I guess I should have figured this out because my parents divorced when I was a baby, and the lack of having my father around left a void in my life.

Going through life sometimes is like connecting the dots where, after something happens, you wonder why events occurred a certain way or why some things never happened at all. In retrospect, I realized I just wasn't equipped to help Kemeil sort through her feelings about her father as I would like to have been. Upon further inspection, I think about how my mother always struggled with inner turmoil rooted in her childhood. My grandmother, too, had a similar story. Only God can help us conquer our inner demons. That's why we need God's Spirit to live in us; to help us overcome our emotional baggage.

In the Shadow of My Daughter's Death

This process doesn't happen overnight. I've learned so much in my many years of going through trails, tribulations, and personal struggles. That's why I have written this book; to share lessons learned and pass them on to someone else. It's not an easy thing to open up and let others know unpleasant details of your life. I know there will be those who judge me greatly about contents I tell in this book. However, if what I share saves one soul, then it will be worth it all.

In 1985. I got married to Kenneth "Kenny" Varner, and for the first time, Kemeil had a father figure in her life. It was just the three of us, and we began adjusting to this new family unit. Less than a year into the marriage, I had another daughter I named Lisa. My husband was delighted to have a daughter of his own, and he gave her plenty of attention. I tried to make us all one family, but once she reached adulthood, Kemeil told me she never felt a part of the family. Back then, she said she would draw pictures of me and Kenny with Lisa on one side and her (by herself) on the opposite side. I never saw those drawings. Words cannot express how hurt I was to hear that. I knew that Kenny favored Lisa because she was the baby, but I didn't know how strongly Kemeil felt.

They did, however, make amends when Kemeil was in the hospital and I was with her. Kenny, whom I had been divorced from, called my phone and spoke to Kemeil through me. He asked for her forgiveness, and he admitted he had not been the father that she deserved. Once I relayed what he said to Kemeil, without hesitation, she gave him a thumbs up (she wasn't talking as much then) as a sign of forgiveness. Truly, this is just another example of how God will intercede in a person's life if they ask Him for help and direction.

Another Adjustment

My marriage lasted only five years. After the separation, I became a single mother to my two beautiful daughters. I did my best to provide for them, raise them, and protect them from the cruel world. I was strict and overprotective because of my personal experiences and fears of what could happen to them. I only let them visit the homes of a few families I knew from church.

Because I was faithful to God and the church, I wanted my girls to have a relationship with Him, too. They were in Sunday School, Youth for Christ services; you name it, and they were there. As young people often do, many times, they didn't agree with attending church so often. Looking back on how I raised them, while I might have tweaked some of my decisions, I don't believe I would have drastically changed much.

Satan the Predator

As my girls grew up in church, they individually received the Holy Ghost. Though this was great news for a young, struggling mother, it didn't mean that the devil wouldn't trouble them. Like I Peter 5:8 says, "Be sober, be vigilant, because your adversary the Devil walketh about as a roaring lion, seeking whom he may devour." (KJV) Satan doesn't care if you go to church. Church attendance doesn't stop him from planting thoughts in your mind. When you listen to him long enough, those thoughts turn into actions. The enemy of our souls seek to destroy all of us, especially the young.

Our family was no different from anyone else. We had financial struggles, emotional battles, and inner spiritual warfare we fought every day. Some of these battles were out in the open and obvious, while many more were hidden and secret. Sadly, Kemeil's troubles were more underneath the surface than I realized. No one can be around their children twenty-four hours a day. We can all remember times when we disobeyed our parents' instructions. There are no perfect children nor perfect parents. We do our best to teach them to do the right things, and at some point, they have to choose which path they will take.

CHAPTER THREE
When Cancer Arrived

I will never, ever, forget this day. Despite my constant insistence, Kemeil avoided going to the doctor for years. When she started having health issues and finally went to be checked out, the doctor found fibroid tumors, and she needed surgery. So, she had the surgery, recuperated, and then went back to work. But within a few years, she continued to have more tumors.

On September 13, 2012, at 32 years old, Kemeil had exploratory surgery. An x-ray had shown another large growth that the doctors could not identify as a fibroid or something else. Out of precaution, Kemeil's gynecologist, who was to perform the surgery, also had an oncologist in the operating room.

Before the surgery, Kemeil feared she needed a total hysterectomy. She wanted to get married in the future and have children. So, right before Kemeil was to be wheeled into the operation room, Lisa and I tried to get Jesus into every bit of our conversations. I mentioned the word "Hell."

"I'm not sure if I believe there is a Hell," Kemeil replied.

I looked at my first-born child as if the Devil himself was speaking through her. I had heard just how much the world had manipulated her mind in believing Hell wasn't real. All my Holy Ghost filled ancestors rose up in me in objection, but I had to pause that debate for another time.

What came out my mouth was, "Kemeil, we are not going to talk about this before you have surgery, but you are in the perfect position to find out if Hell is real or not! We will continue this discussion at another time if you make it through this surgery."

I mentioned earlier that Kemeil received the Holy Ghost at a young age. But, since then, she had strayed from the Lord. The world and its attractions had strongly wrapped its fingers around her heart. We had good reason to be worried about Kemeil's survival during the surgery. We knew she wasn't in right standing with God. We were concerned about her body, yes, but also the condition of her soul.

Lisa and I stayed in hospital's waiting room during Kemeil's surgery. As we waited, we prayed that God would successfully bring my daughter through the surgery. The hours stretched out so long that Lisa and I decided to go to the hospital cafeteria to eat. While we were still there, Kemeil's doctor came in to talk with us. His next words are embedded in my memory. Almost holding my breath, I asked him how Kemeil was doing.

"She's in recovery," he said.

"Does she still have her uterus?" I asked him. "Yes," he responded.

I breathed a sigh of relief only to hear him say, "Her uterus is the least of our concerns."

From that moment on, our world changed forever.

The doctor grabbed a napkin and began to draw pictures of what they found and what organs they had to remove from Kemeil's body. The tumor was the size of a human head, and when they cut it open, they found cancerous cells. At the time, I was not familiar with the word, "metastasized," but he used it to tell us that the cancer had remained in the tumor. They had removed an ovary, her appendix, a fallopian tube, and film from her chest.

Lisa did not say a word. Later, she'd admit to panicking because she thought I was going to freak out, and she wouldn't have known what to do. Usually, Kemeil would be the one to calm me when I got upset. Thanks to God, I remained composed. We listened to everything the doctor had to say including that going forward Kemeil would now be in the hands of the oncologist.

When Lisa and I were allowed to see Kemeil in the recovery area, I thought the doctors had already told her the findings of her surgery. They had not. She told us that the doctors had said everything was fine, and the tumor wasn't cancerous. I looked at the nurse, then Lisa, and I had to tell my thirty- two-year-old first born child that she had cancer.

"Am I dying?" she asked me.

The nurse told her no, she was not dying.

After Lisa and I were left alone with her, Kemeil told us she had prayed to God before she went into surgery. Remember, this was the same person who told me before surgery she wasn't sure if she believed there was a Hell. Look how minds change when Death's shadow is in the room with you! One of the bargains she made with God was, if he gave her another chance to live, she would find a church that she preferred to attend.

Praise God, this was welcomed news! Kemeil stayed in the hospital for approximately five days. The following next months were filled with many doctor's appointments, discussions, and decisions. Kemeil had to take six rounds of chemo; her first one was on December 21, 2012; seven days before her 33rd birthday.

CHAPTER FOUR

Without Peace

In reading through my old prayer journals, I ran across an entry from August of 2015. I wrote, "No matter what happened in Kemeil's life, she was never happy for long. You would think that just being alive each day when you were diagnosed with cancer would bring thankfulness; but it didn't." I wrote about how Kemeil complained all the time about one thing or another. When she told me she was miserable at work and wanted a new job, I prayed that God would grant her request. When she complained that she was overlooked for a promotion with more pay, I prayed for that to happen. When she decided to move out of the house to Philadelphia, I prayed that she would find an apartment. Each time I prayed, the Lord granted our petitions. But did Kemeil thank God for those blessings? Honestly, I believe she did, but then she complained about the new job, the new apartment, and still was trying to get a better salary.

The truth about Kemeil's problems were that she didn't have peace with God. No peace with God meant she didn't have peace with anything else in her life. Isaiah 9:6 says that He (Jesus) shall be called the Prince of Peace. (KJV) When we have God in our hearts, *He* gives us peace. There are many storms, struggles, trials, and tests we go through in this life. But in John 16:33, Jesus says, "these things I have spoken unto you, that *in me* ye might have peace. In the world ye shall have tribulation:

but be of good cheer; I have overcome the world." (KJV) If you once knew God and you walked away from Him, you are left defenseless from the attacks of the devil. This means that Satan has free course to attack your mind any time and in any way he wants to.

Trouble reached far into Kemeil's life – so far that she thought of committing suicide multiple times. When Kemeil was twelve years old, I had scolded her for something she had done. I walked away from her and headed towards my bedroom when God impressed upon me to return to her. I found her in the kitchen with a steak knife in her hand testing how sharp the point was. I was shocked, hugged her, and spoke kind words to her. But, in all honesty, I thought she was just trying to make me feel bad about yelling at her. I didn't think about it anymore after that. It wasn't until Kemeil, in her adulthood, confessed that she thought of and had planned to kill herself on several occasions.

On one of those occasions, she confessed to being in the basement of our house with a line of pills she planned to take. Where had she gotten those pills? Kemeil, at that time, didn't take medicine. Thank God! He used a stranger, someone Kemeil had just met the night before at a party, to stop her from taking them! She was just about to swallow them when her phone rang. Peter invited her to go with him to Fire Island. Neither of them had any idea how God had touched this young man's heart to call her at that moment! I would have been devastated, inconsolable, and have blamed myself forever if I had found that Kemeil took her own life. Thank you, Jesus, for your mercy and for working in mysterious ways, Hallelujah!

Liar!

The devil is not a nice guy! He uses every opportunity, every disappointment, and every emotion to get you off course. What he doesn't tell you is that when you're not covered by the Blood of Jesus; when you don't have the spirit of God living in you (the Holy Ghost) to fight against those attacks on your mind, you're just like roadkill. Satan runs you over, and he leaves you feeling like your only recourse is to kill yourself.

If Satan gets your mind, then he's got you! He tells you how much you have messed up. He says no one loves you, not even God. He tells you things would be better if you were dead. **ALL SATAN EVER TELLS YOU ARE LIES!!!!!** In John 8:44. Jesus said, "Ye are of your father the devil, and the lusts of your father ye will do. He was a murderer from the beginning, and abode not in the truth, because there is no truth in him. When he speaketh a lie, he speaketh of his own: for he is a liar, and the father of it." (KJV)

As the children's song says, "Jesus loves me this I know/For the Bible tells me so/Little ones to Him belong/They are weak, but He is strong/Yes, Jesus loves me..." No one loves you is a lie! John 3:16 says, "For God so loved the world, that he gave his only begotten Son, that whosoever, believeth in him should not perish, but have everlasting life." (KJV) Oh, how I wished so many famous people could have been reached before they took their own lives -- actors, chefs, fashion designers, singers, and the list goes on. Depression doesn't discriminate. The young, the old, the rich, and the poor all commit suicide every day. The raw truth is this – even those who profess to be Christians. That's why it's so important that we cling to Jesus by reading His Word daily, staying before God in prayer, and resisting the devil and he shall flee – James 4:7. (KJV)

Reflections

During Kemeil's recuperation periods, we spent many hours talking. She asked me questions and cried often in regret of past decisions. She also promised to make better life choices once she recovered. What I find interesting is that when some people feel they are close to death, they will promise to do anything for God to get another chance at life. They make all kinds of bargains, or so they think, with the Lord only to keep none of them once they receive what they want. Such was the case with Kemeil. She kept the same pattern after each time she had surgery – expressing regrets during recuperation, talking of changing bad behaviors, and promising to head in the right direction towards God once she got better. Then....as soon as she felt well enough to drive, she headed straight toward the bar and ungodly company.

Kemeil once confessed that after she had hernia surgery, while she still had drainage bulbs hanging from her body, she had driven herself to the bar for a drink. I couldn't believe my ears! However, it was just further evidence of how Satan only cares about one thing, our destruction!

Warnings

During these emotional talks with Kemeil, I was amazed at how many warnings God sent her way that she never told me about. He had given her many chances to change her ways throughout her life.

I want to pause here for a moment. So often, we, as parents, pray for our wayward children, but we see little evidence that those prayers are working. Now I realize that God is working behind the scenes when we pray for our children or any individual. He sends warnings, dreams, and even people in answer to our fervent prayers. But we cannot override a person's will. God does not force anyone to serve Him no matter how passionate someone prays for them to do so.

However, God still moves because of our prayers, and He can touch a person's heart. So, continue praying and believing in God, that He can get their attention long enough to soften their hearts to listen to what He is trying to tell them.

One day, Kemeil told me a story of what happened to her one evening. She was coming home from college and was waiting for a train at the station. A woman she did not know kept trying to approach her and speak with her. Kemeil tried to get rid of the woman, but she was insistent that they talk. Finally, Kemeil relented.

The woman told her these words. "Because you don't believe the Lord, you're going to suffer many things."

Then the woman left without another word. Kemeil didn't see where she went. Those prophetic words from years ago painfully came true and haunted her mind for the rest of her life.

God also warned my daughter through her dreams. In one of them, she was in a crowd of saints from the church that she knew. They passed her while she walked in the opposite direction.

Someone in the dream yelled to her, "You're going the wrong way!"

A song by Alan Jackson comes to my mind that says, "softly and tenderly Jesus is calling/calling O sinner come home." Is Jesus speaking to you who are reading this right now? How many times have you ignored His pleading? We pay a great price when we ignore the small, still- voiced warnings of the Lord.

Kemeil would agree with me, if she were here to tell you.

Two Masters

Once she recovered, although Kemeil went back to work and her usual routines, she did keep the promise to find a church. However, she picked and chose how she would keep that promise. She served on the usher board, sang in the choir, and she assisted the pastor. But she also continued to break God's commandments.

Bible scriptures speak of good kings who did not remove the "high places" (pagan shrines). If we don't totally repent of our sins and turn away from them (while asking God to help us), Satan uses them as stronghold under which to operate, and we are never totally free as we claim to be.

Kemeil wanted God and the world at the same time. Sin's pleasures are enjoyable, but like some car lease agreements, there is a huge balloon payment due at the end. The Bible calls it judgement. God won't take second place in our lives, and He refuses to be a weekend God --in other words, when we only serve Him on a part-time basis (Sundays) and whenever it's convenient for us. The Word declares that we cannot serve two masters.

Satan paints a pretty picture of what it is like to follow him, and he makes great promises. But what he doesn't tell you is that there are always strings attached to choosing his ways. Always read the fine print of a contract. God's Word clearly points out what happens when we agree to Satan's terms.

Human nature (our sinful nature) doesn't want to be told what to do. No rules, no laws, no restrictions. Just let live and let others live the way they want to. Sounds appealing, right? Well, the problem with that is in the fine print. For every bad choice we make, there are consequences.

Kemeil made bad choices and it cost her life.

CHAPTER FIVE
From Bad, To Worse, To God in PA

To pursue a better job opportunity, Kemeil moved to Harrisburg, PA on September 14, 2015. With that promotion came more stress and her illness grew worse; but Kemeil kept a lot of that from me.

On Christmas Eve that same year, she came home to New York to stay with me and Lisa. We enjoyed having her home. My mother came over for Christmas Day, and we had lots of fun together as a family.

Before Kemeil had come home, I had an unusual dream about her, and I pondered it's meaning. However, I wouldn't have to wait long for its interpretation.

For some reason I didn't go to bed at my usual time that Christmas evening. I was awake when, after midnight, Kemeil came to my room, lifted her shirt, and put my hand on a mass (a little bigger than the size of a golf ball). She really wasn't going to tell me about it, but the weight of fear finally became too much. She confessed to having felt the lump almost a month prior. She didn't want to acknowledge the possibility that cancer had returned. Thinking back on the dream God gave me, I realized that He was warning me that something was wrong. In it, I saw a text message from Kemeil with the number twenty-six. It was early the morning of December 26 when she showed me the mass.

After hearing the news, I tried my best to comfort Kemeil while encouraging her to get checked out by a doctor. It had been almost three years since she had to deal with cancer. I told her to inform her new pastor about it and have him and his wife pray for her.

When Kemeil moved, I held her up in prayer, but I also recognized that she needed consistent spiritual guidance and a group of believers to support her where she lived. She initially had a hard time finding the right fit, but eventually God led her to a loving congregation. That's where she met Bishop and Mother Screven of the Emmanuel Church of God in Christ in PA. She also met Mother Finesse Cobb, a wonderful woman of God who would become a second mother to Kemeil, and a kind-hearted saint of a woman named Kam Fine.

In Romans 11:33 it says "…his ways past finding out." (KJV) We often say God works in mysterious ways. Kemeil didn't know anyone in Pennsylvania, and we didn't have any relatives there nor did she have any friends. She thought the only reason she had moved was because of a manager's position; but God had other plans in mind.

God had been trying to get Kemeil's attention for years. She knew this. No matter how she tried to ignore God's still, small voice, His presence always presented itself no matter where she went. Psalms 139:8 says, "If I ascend up into heaven, thou art there: if I make my bed in hell, behold, thou art there." (KJV)

None of us can hide from God. He sees us in the dark the same as He sees us in the light. When God has a plan and a purpose for your life, running from that plan can be very costly. Remember Jonah who ran from what God told him to do? He ended up in the belly of a large fish.

As Kemeil's illness grew worse, so did the reality that the God she had avoided was the same God that she desperately needed. What do you do when the doctor's news is all bad? She was a healthy, vibrant, ambitious, young lady one day, but then the tables turned drastically.

On March 9, 2016, Kemeil gave me the news. The cancer had returned, and she needed a second surgery. That surgery took place on April 5, 2016. This time, Kemeil only stayed in the hospital for a few days. She pleaded with her doctors to allow her to go home to be present for a surprise proposal that her sister Lisa was going to get from her boyfriend, Harold.

Soon afterwards, Lisa asked Kemeil to be the maid of honor and despite her illness, she agreed to take on those duties. By the grace of God, Kemeil did an excellent job as maid of honor, and she attended the wedding on October 8, 2016.

Trying To Make It Work

For a while, it seemed as if Kemeil could skip chemotherapy. However, those hopes were smashed when on June 30, 2016, she was told that she had spots on her lungs. That September,

Kemeil started her second round of treatments. The chemo continued until February of 2017. But unfortunately, four months later, Kemeil had to endure another chemo round.

Despite chemo treatments, Kemeil tried hard to live a normal life. She continued to work, enrolled in college, and attended church when her health allowed. But the side effects of the treatments took their toll. She often got very sick at work to where she couldn't keep food in her stomach. The only thing she could tolerate all day was lactose-free milk. She lost all her hair and a lot of weight.

The Only Option

In November of 2017, Mother Finesse called me to say Kemeil was extremely sick and refused to go to the hospital. She really needed me to come to Pennsylvania. After much talking, I finally persuaded my daughter to go to the emergency room.

Her argument against going was that none of the doctors she had seen were able to help improve her condition. The chemo was not working. She needed specialized care, and she was too weak to get it done alone.

Sometimes you need an advocate to help fight your battles. Kemeil had tried all she could to get better by herself, but she needed me to help care for her. She didn't want me to know everything about her health because she knew I would worry. It was difficult for me to help her from New York while she was a state away in Pennsylvania. Not everything could be accomplished over the phone. But things were at a critical level, so I had to step in.

Once Kemeil was admitted into the hospital, her sister, Lisa, brother-in-law, Harold, and I came as often as we could. I remember when I walked into Kemeil's room seeing how glad she was that I was there.

Even with anti-nausea meds, she still threw up every time she tried to eat. Other parts of her body broke down, and she experienced anxiety attacks. The sicker Kemeil got, the more she confessed what was wrong with her. She had developed diabetes and denied having it for a year. Her body had problems with infections, but she wouldn't go to a specialist to get checked out.

"If I ignored these issues," she told me, "I thought they would go away by themselves."

I knew the real reason she wouldn't go was that she feared she was worse than she wanted to admit.

By the second day of her emergency room visit, Kemeil was admitted to Penn State Health Milton Hershey Medical Center. They performed a battery of tests. None of the results were good. During the thirty-four days she was in the hospital, the cancer continued spreading throughout her body. She was too sick to continue chemo. Almost a week later, on November 20, she found out she had five inoperable brain tumors.

Despite the grim outlook, I did whatever I could to make her comfortable. When I saw she wouldn't eat her food, I fed her.

Lisa and Harold did what they could as well. One day, when Mother Finesse came to visit, Kemeil couldn't stop throwing up. She didn't have any food in her so all that came up was green bile. Gently weeping, Lisa began to sing "Yes, Jesus Loves Me," which was one of Kemeil's favorite songs. We all joined in, sang, prayed, and wept.

Every day was extremely difficult with a new health challenge. My daughter had become a human pin cushion. They stuck her for blood samples, to administer medicine through an IV, and to give shots. The doctors delivered painful news.

Death's shadow was everywhere.

CHAPTER SIX

Released

A pressure cooker is a sealed chamber that traps the steam it generates to heat its contents. As the steam builds, pressure increases and drives the temperature inside past 212 degrees Fahrenheit.

Like the steam in a pressure cooker, our emotions can reach a boiling point. Family disputes, job loss, a failed marriage, drug use, death, abuse, financial problems, etc. can push us over the edge.

Because of her strong mistrust of people, Kemeil, for most of her life, tried to deal with unresolved issues alone. On the outside, she could look tough, but on the inside, she needed help. When her health rapidly failed, she realized that she needed to pour out her soul to someone who would keep what she said in confidence.

That person was Bishop Allen Roach.

Kemeil became acquainted with Bishop Roach through her sister, Lisa, and brother-in-law Harold. He was their pastor. She had previously attended a few church services at Newborn Light House in Maryland. Slowly, Kemeil grew to be fond of him, his wife, and the saints there. When she discovered that he provided counselling services, she reached out to him.

Throughout Kemeil's fight with cancer, Bishop Roach made time to talk with her whenever she was able. Mostly, she just wanted a listening ear, an understanding heart, and wise counsel. One day, after she was hospitalized, Bishop and Mother Roach made a trip to visit her. They had only intended to stay for an hour or so but ended up staying much longer. During their visit, Kemeil unloaded things that had heavily weighed on her heart for years. Though she shed many tears, she finally found release.

Many things can keep us in mental bondage, like unforgiveness, bitterness, anger, grudges, and resentment, and they can keep us from moving successfully forward in our lives. It is well known that stress is unhealthy. Too much stress can wear you down and make you sick, both mentally and physically. Stress can be linked to an array of conditions like heart attacks, high blood pressure, and stroke.

James 5:16 says "Confess your faults one to another, and pray one for another, that ye may be healed. The effectual fervent prayer of a righteous man availeth much." (KJV) Kemeil had not forgiven others who had offended her, and she had become bitter and angry because of it. She was disappointed that life hadn't turned out for her how she imagined it should have, and she blamed many others for her setbacks. She very much needed to let God heal her hurts and the only way to do that was to allow forgiveness into her heart.

The first step was to let it out, and then the healing could begin. Bishop and Mother Roach provided the outlet Kemeil needed.

Before her life ended, I asked her "Can you forgive all those who have offended you throughout your life?"

"Yes," she answered.

It's so important that we forgive one another. I didn't say it was easy to do, but it is a requirement from the Lord if we are to go to heaven. Jesus said in Matthew 6:14-15 For if ye forgive men their trespasses, your heavenly father will also forgive you: But if ye forgive not men their trespasses, neither will your father forgive your trespasses." (KJV)

We have often heard it said that forgiveness frees you. The Devil tells us that the offender is getting away from punishment. The real fact is that we are punishing ourselves by constantly remembering the offense. The memories don't make us happy, but angrier. Trust me, I know what I'm saying; been there – done that! It is a constant battle with the flesh to forgive *but with God's help*, it can be done.

I praise God that Kemeil was set free in the end!

My Strength For The Journey

Though I walked through that hospital so many times in despair, I clung to Jesus for strength. I quickly found the chapel and poured out my heart to God every day. I placed Kemeil's name on the prayer list every time I went. I didn't know what

God would do, heal her or take her, but until His will was done, I kept on praying.

I'm grateful to God for His strength and those He sent to strengthen me. If I were to start listing names, I would leave someone out; so, I'll go another route. In addition to family members that I spoke to just about every day, I had those who purposely called me every night when I got to Kemeil's townhouse for the evening. Those angels will never know how much of a comfort that was to me. I would be drained after trying to stay upbeat for Kemeil while I was with her. Sometimes, it was just a day of bad news and tears between the two of us, but God always had someone to hold the family up in prayers and encourage me.

I had close friends who I could call at any time. I had wonderful Sisters in Christ who would travel to come see Kemeil in the hospital. They would comfort her, and that allowed me time to take a break. I thank God for giving me favor with the nursing staff who gave me free food vouchers every day. In December of 2017, I received a greeting card with money in it from the nurses. I was so touched, They knew that I was taking an Uber rideshare back and forth from the hospital (unless someone gave me a ride back to Kemeil's house). They all signed the card with encouragement. God is a provider!

Even though my pastor, Doug Davis of Bethel UPC of Westbury, New York, couldn't come to see Kemeil in person, he had his assistant arrange for another young pastor, and his wife who worked at the same hospital in Pennsylvania, to meet us.

Look at God! Many saints from so many churches gave and supported us in any way they could. Even on my job, people were understanding of my situation and spoke comforting words to me.

I want to also say a special thank you to Elder David Gillespie and his family. He was a great encouragement to Kemeil. I can never thank him enough for his kindness.

Time To Say I Love You

Going back and forth from New York to Pennsylvania wasn't easy for me. I don't drive on highways, and so driving myself to Pennsylvania was not an option. I used Amtrak Railways to travel there and stayed at Kemeil's townhouse. During the time she was in the hospital, I used my sick days from work to visit her. I could only stay a few days at a time, and then, I would have to go back to work.

I was under a lot of pressure at work because of all the days I had taken off. I had booked a train ticket for the morning of November 28,, 2017, but on November 27, the Human Resources Manager told me that while I could take FMLA (Family and Medical Leave Act) days off, I wouldn't get paid for them. He said I had to be the one sick to get paid. I was in tears at my desk. I couldn't afford to miss two weeks of pay from my check, which would equal an entire pay period. I prayed to God for guidance and then talked to some friends.

They told me what to do: leave work immediately and go to the doctor for an excused absence letter.

I got an emergency appointment with my doctor that day, and when he took my blood pressure, it was over 170. Before he read my vital signs, he was giving me a hard time about writing the letter. He was only going to give me a week's absence. However, when he saw how high my pressure was, he was alarmed and took it again in his office. Then, his fingers flew across the keyboard. He had typed an order for two weeks' absence.

He asked me all sorts of questions, "Are you dizzy?" Do you have a headache?" I didn't feel sick just overwhelmed. I broke down crying in his office. He had never seen me like that. He ordered the nurse to give me additional tests, but then, when the results were all negative, he let me leave with the letter I needed.

Can you believe that God used my high blood pressure to get what I needed? That's exactly what happened. Not only did I get two weeks leave, but I was prescribed anxiety medicine as well. I didn't question God nor the doctor. The more he wrote on my letter, the better it was for me. I had experienced problems sleeping, so I accepted the anxiety medication.

I left to be with Kemeil on November 28, and stayed with her until December 15,. During this time, we expressed how we really felt about each other. It was a gift from God that before she departed this life, we got to say all we wanted to tell one another.

Some days she was talkative, and other days she wasn't. The doctors decided to attempt to shrink her brain tumors with radiation. The first treatment was on December 11. There were side effects of these treatments, like short term

memory loss. She would forget what happened the day before. Another was hallucinations -- she saw things that weren't there, like bugs, papers flying across the room, and cake floating in the air.

Lisa and I had a theory. Occasionally, Kemeil seemed to be a happy pre-teen. She would talk about simple things like cake and other goodies she wanted to eat. But then, there were times she was the depressed thirty-seven-year-old afraid of dying. In one conversation, she apologized for not meeting my expectations and turning out the way she did.

"Kemeil, you are my beautiful, highly intelligent, ambitious, and caring daughter," I told her. "You looked out for me because you were the eldest. Whatever concerned me, you did your best to help. I love you just the way you are, and I've always been proud of you."

One of those moments where she looked out for me was when she had lost her voice for some unexplained reason, and she could only talk in a whisper. Kemeil insisted that I get renter's insurance on my apartment that I had moved to after selling my house. On a three-way phone conversation with an agent, she made sure I got that coverage.

"Don't worry, I'll get that later," I told her about the insurance. She disagreed. "Let's do this now while I got some kind of voice."

In return, Kemeil told me how much she admired and appreciated me. She said that, other than God, I was her everything. When I think back to those precious moments with a knot in my throat and tears threatening to roll, I think "Isn't that just like God!" We didn't spend those intimate moments bashing each other or bringing up painful memories. Instead, we spent them expressing love for each other.

Doesn't God treat us the same way? When we come contrite to Him, He doesn't beat us over the head with our sins. That's what Satan does! God forgives us and tells us that we can get up and go forward with His direction and help.

I'm so grateful God gave us that time together. Things could have been a lot different. God could have taken her the moment she was diagnosed with cancer. She could have died on the operation table during any one of her many surgeries. But instead, we had six years and time at the end to say, "I love you."

CHAPTER SEVEN

God So Loved Kemeil

Engrafted in this story, were special moments when God expressed His love for Kemeil through my lips and gave me the exact, unrehearsed words she needed to hear. This event happened before she was admitted into the hospital.

Your Heavenly Father (September 10, 2017)

I had gone to a prayer service here in New York, and I got a call from Kemeil who was in Pennsylvania. She was greatly distraught and sounded like she was at the end of her rope. She was sick, couldn't keep anything in her stomach, and alone in her apartment. I abruptly left the prayer service, and while I was driving back home, we talked. I parked outside of my apartment and continued to talk to her in the car. I told Kemeil that God did love her, and He had great plans for her. However, she must acknowledge that she needed God to take control of her life.

This also meant she had to admit she was wrong in not following Christ. "Do you talk to God?" I asked Kemeil.

"I'm afraid to," she replied. "Why are you afraid?"

"Because," she admitted, "I'm afraid of what he might say."

With great compassion, I explained that God was her heavenly Father. Just like she knew I loved her because she was my daughter no matter what she did, so did her heavenly Father love her regardless of what has happened. He only wanted what's best for her, and He's waiting with open arms for her to come back to Him.

After talking a bit, I asked Kemeil if she was ready to let God back into her life.

"Yes," she said.

"Are you sure? I don't want you to just say it for my sake. Make a conscious decision that this is what you want. Is it?"

"Yes," she repeated.

I told her to pray to God out loud while we were both on the phone. I knew she expected me to pray but I also knew that it was very important that she spoke to God herself.

What she said surprised me.

"I am so, so, sorry! I thought I could do things on my own. I thought I could get what I wanted without you, but I can't! I tried all my life to live without you, but I'm so, so tired. I can't do this anymore!" Then she added, "God, I'm not asking for but one thing; whether I die the next minute, or tomorrow, or in a week; I'm just asking that whenever you take me, my soul is right with you."

After her heartfelt plea to God for forgiveness, I took over the prayer. I pleaded the blood of Jesus over every foul spirit that had possession of Kemeil. I called them all out by name: suicide, depression, lust, alcoholism, and sickness. I told Satan to take his filthy hands off my daughter's mind in Jesus' name!

I told Satan to get out of my daughter's house and go back to the pit of Hell!

Over the phone, I heard Kemeil screaming to the top of her lungs. I believed with all my heart that the Lord was freeing her right then and there. When I finished the prayer, I told Kemeil, "Welcome back!" I said that God would show her how to walk before Him from that point, and that I would continue to pray that God lead and guide her what to do. Then, I told her that she had to get rid of the alcohol in her cabinet.

In Matthew 3:8 it says, "Bring forth therefore fruits meet for repentance." (KJV) In other words, she had to be serious in walking away from a sinful life. I knew Kemeil had alcohol in her house, and that it was a temptation for her to get drunk when she felt depressed. So, I told her to get rid of it. On the spot, I heard her go to the cabinet and then go to the sink. One by one she poured out all the bottles as she sang the hymn "My Sins are Blotted Out I Know."

I went on to advise her to separate herself from this one friend that was no good for her. I only met this young woman one time, face-to-face, and I knew she was a messenger of Satan. This person attached herself to Kemeil, persuaded her to go in the wrong direction, and involved Kemeil in her own dramas. God had given me a dream about the young lady before I ever met her, but I didn't know that until I told Kemeil the dream.

As I laid out what I had seen, Kemeil got very quiet. Little did I know I had described this young lady exactly how she looked in person. It wasn't until a conversation with Kemeil weeks later that she confessed it was her friend.

After she recommitted her life to Christ, the very next day, Kemeil was visited by this person. I was nervous, and Kemeil knew it. But she reassured me that she was ready to change her life.

"Don't worry Ma," she said. "It's not that kind of party."

She wasn't going to let that person take her back to previous behaviors. September 10, 2017 was the beginning of Kemeil coming back home to Jesus; Glory to God!

Let's Have Church! (December 10, 2017)

During Kemeil's stay at Penn State Hospital, she wanted someone to read the Bible to her, teach her, and to attend church.

One of the nurses, who took special interest in her and befriended me, read her the Bible for an hour. God used people all over the hospital to encourage Kemeil, and I can never thank God enough for them.

One day, Kemeil begged me to let her go to church. I felt so sorry for her. At that point, she couldn't even walk by herself, but she pleaded for me to take her to church.

So, my mind came up with a plan! I called Lisa and Harold and told them, "My baby wants to go to church, and church she will have!"

The three of us came up with an entire service. We had a choir march song ("There's a Feeling in the Air…"), and an opening prayer and scripture (Psalms 15). There was devotional service with songs and testimonies (Lisa and I). We had another choir selection, and then our speaker for that Sunday was Harold.

When I told Harold about being the speaker a few days prior to our service, he knew I was serious. He prayed to God about what to say. I woke up that Sunday morning, and I happened to peek in their room at Kemeil's townhouse. Harold was awake. Later, when I returned, Harold was asleep again. That was interesting. It wasn't until we were with Kemeil that I realized what had happened. Harold let us know that he didn't know what to say.

"I've never dealt with anyone who had cancer before," he told Kemeil, "and I didn't want to just make something up. God awakened me early this morning and gave me words to say."

Silent, Kemeil lay in the bed and listened. Harold said that God gave him the topic, "It's not about this life.": He spoke about Lazarus (John 11), and even though Jesus raised Lazarus from the dead, Lazarus still had to die a second time.

"I don't know whether God will heal you or take you," he said, "but the most important thing was that you are right with the Lord. We love you, and even if you pass, we will be comforted as long as we know we will see you again in Heaven."

In his message, Harold emphasized that we, as humans, try so hard to hold on to this life. But what matters the most is the afterlife and where we will spend eternity. I thank God for using Harold on that day. Kemeil received what he said and clapped her hands when he was done. We ended our hospital service with the song by Bishop Paul Morton: "Get the Glory."

What I also found interesting about that day was not one nurse came into the room during this time. We had a whole service with singing, hand clapping, and tambourine beating, but no one disturbed us. In fact, when we opened the door to the room, some nurses clapped and said they enjoyed the service.

Look at God! Lisa and I said if Harold ever got called to the ministry, we had heard his first sermon with Kemeil.

Faith At The Window (December 13, 2017)

According to one of my journal entries, Kemeil made her peace with God on this date when she had been admitted to Penn State Hospital in Pennsylvania.

I was encouraged by a nurse who did not work at Penn State to get Kemeil out the bed. I asked a hospital nurse to help me get her to a chair by the window. It took us a long time to accomplish this task since Kemeil's legs couldn't support her weight. Once we got her situated, I went to leave out the room, but something inside me made me turn back.

Kemeil had stopped talking. She was clearly afraid and depressed.

"Kemeil, you have not spoken for three days," I said. "I need to know what's on your mind. I need to know from you what you want? If you tell me, you are tired of living like this and just want to be with Jesus, then I will accept that. Kemeil, I will be okay if that's what you want. But if you tell me, you want to keep fighting to live, then we will keep on fighting and praying!"

"I want to live," she said.

"Okay," I responded, "then we will keep believing the Lord!" But then, I saw this sadness in her face. "Believe God for forgiveness."

To my shock, she said, "How can I?"

I then realized what the Devil had been doing. He had convinced her that she was too far gone and had done too many things in her life to be forgiven by God. I then got a righteous indignation against that Devil! I took for granted that, because Kemeil grew up in the church, she knew how to get to God once she made up her mind to return. What I didn't count on was how strong the guilt played on her mind.

So, then I understood what she was afraid of. That Devil had talked to her night and day. He had told her over and over that she was just going to die and go to Hell!

This was the second time God gave me the exact words needed to say. I had her to look me in the face.

"Kemeil," I said, "the Bible says that all have sinned and come short of the Glory of God. That includes me. None of us are without sin! Christ died on the cross for our sins; He took our place, and all we have to do is ask God to forgive us and He does."

God's plan is very simple: repent and turn from our sinful ways. Man would have us go through hoops and do somersaults, but not God! Once you have truly repented, asked God to come into your heart, and believe that He will guide you through the process of salvation (Ac. 2:38 KJV) – that's it!"

I continued to follow God's leading, and I told my daughter to talk to me as if I was God Himself. Although she had repented a few months ago, I asked her to repeat the following: "God, I repent of all my sins, and I want you to restore me to a right relationship with you."

"Talk to me," I said, "Look at me as if God was standing before you – out loud so I can hear what you're saying."

She intensely looked at me and said, "God, I'm thirty-seven years old, but I never knew you. I want to see your Glory. I want to know what it means to know you, Lord."

I put my hand in the middle of her chest. "Kemeil, I don't know when or how God is going to do it. I don't know if He is going to heal you or take you. But God is going to let us both know that it is well with your soul."

The entire day, I had felt such heaviness., Once I said those words, I experienced a flood of peace washing over me like sunrays from Heaven!

"I feel so much better," I told her. "I do, too," she responded.

We both went into praise before the Lord. I saw God's peace on my daughter's face like I had never seen before. Oh praise God for that awesome day of deliverance!

CHAPTER EIGHT
Silver Springs

Three days later, on December 16, 2017, Kemeil was transferred from Penn State Hospital in Pennsylvania to Manor Care Silver Springs Nursing facility in Maryland. The hospital released her because there wasn't anything else the doctors could do, and she was in no shape to return home. Lisa, Harold, and I had discussed a plan going forward how to care for her once she was dismissed from Penn State. It was a very difficult decision.

Although my mother was in a nursing home, I cared for her, and I still had to work. My apartment was small and couldn't accommodate Kemeil's medical needs. So, Lisa and Harold agreed to see to her care in Maryland. I can't express enough times what this meant to me. They had only been married for a little over a year, and they both agreed to take on this challenging duty. The Silver Springs Nursing facility was the closest place to their home and was the only place that accepted Kemeil because of her condition.

On the day she arrived to Silver Springs, Lisa and Harold went to the facility to meet her. They frequently visited her and so did different saints from the New Born Light House congregation, including Elder David Gillispie. They played the card game UNO, and in spite of Kemeil having brain tumors, she beat him often. Elder Gillispie created a wall-sized photo gallery for her. It was a combination of scriptures, family pictures, and word sayings to cheer her up and remind her that she was greatly loved. Since I could not be there at the time, I stayed in contact with Kemeil via phone. It was comforting for me to know that she was surrounded by family and friends who could check up on her often in Maryland.

Ten days later, I saw Kemeil. When I got to her room, I had to pretend not to be shocked by how much weight she had lost. When I talked with her nurses, they said she only ate a few bites of food a day. The heavy medication caused her constipation and kept her in constant pain. Then, they had to give her something to force her to move her bowels. This constant cycle went on until the end. Nevertheless, we tried to keep her as cheerful as possible.

Thursday, December 28, 2017, was Kemeil's 38th birthday. It would be the last one she celebrated. I bought her a gift, balloons, and cupcakes with candles. Lisa, Harold, and I sang "Happy Birthday," and then she blew out the candles. She tried to play UNO with us, but her severe back pain made her stop. Elder Gillispie had given her a back massager to use, and I tried to massage her back with it, but it didn't relieve the pain. She suffered all day until the nurses could give her another stool softer. She was on so much medication, they had to wait a certain length of time before she could take anything else.

By the time the medicine worked, it was time for us to leave for the day. I had to go home the next day. I was so upset on the train ride back. Anytime I left her, I never knew if that would be the last time. My mind and emotions were always split in two. On the one hand, I was trying to believe God that He would heal her. But on the other hand, I was trying to accept the worst- case scenario.

While Kemeil was in Silver Springs, her condition took a turn for the worst. Her legs were swollen, and liquid soaked through the socks she had on. I had thought it was another blood clot (like she had in the hospital), but when Kemeil was sent for testing, the results came back that the cancer had spread to her pelvis.

I Surrender All In The I.C.U.

I used a few of my sick days to visit Kemeil after New Year's Day, 2018. By the time I returned home on January 3, I got a call from Lisa. The nursing home had sent Kemeil to the Adventist HealthCare Hospital emergency room. The hospital then admitted her to the I.C.U, and on January 8, 2018, I made my way back to Maryland.

When I first saw Kemeil hooked up to all those incessantly beeping machines, I struggled to keep my hopes alive. I didn't know what else to say to my baby. I just did what I knew how to do – pray! I found the chapel and laid out on the floor. I asked God to help me, to have mercy on Kemeil, to help our family that had to go through this nightmare. Whenever I went to see her, I dreaded turning the corner, because I thought at any moment, a doctor was going to meet me with the news that Kemeil was gone.

She had no appetite, so she received nourishment through IVs. Because the cancer had spread throughout her body, she couldn't be fed through tubes because of the infection risk.

At this point, her life was in the hands of the Lord.

I did everything I could think of to help. I bought a CD player and continuously played sermons. I found blood on her face from where she pulled the air tubes from her nose. I cleaned her face and fingernails which were encrusted with blood. I rubbed her head with blessed olive oil per her request. I massaged her feet although her toenails were crusted with fungus. Mostly I just held her hand and prayed.

Doctors and nurses regularly checked on her. One young doctor came to talk to us. As she talked, she cried and told her how sorry she was that Kemeil would never get married like her sister or have children. She also listed a number of things Kemeil would never experience.

I was mortified!

This doctor was falling apart at the wrong time and in the I.C.U. of all places! I quickly ended the conversation. Here I was trying with every ounce of my strength left to keep Kemeil encouraged, and this poor doctor was doing damage.

That's when the Lord took over.

When I got the doctor out the room, I felt an urgency from the Lord to act immediately. "Kemeil, we are from this moment focusing on the here and now," I told her. "We are leaving the past in the past!"

Regrets had gripped both of us long enough. We didn't have any more time to waste. Kemeil nodded her head in agreement with me.

The Lord then took over my tongue and my mind. It was like an out-of- body experience. I saw a vision of Christ in the Garden of Gethsemane, sweating as if bleeding, asking His father to take the metaphorical cup of suffering from Him. I held my daughter's hand and said that there was just one more thing she needed to do – surrender her will to God.

I was shocked with the words that was coming out of my mouth! Inside I was thinking "Who said that?"

"I know you're scared." I told her what I saw in my mind. "All of us who love you and are praying for you fear the worst could happen. We want God to heal you, raise you up, and allow you to be the great witness that you can be after this. But that's our own will."

"We have to yield to God's will. Our plan A is healing for you. But God's plan A may be to free you from all this pain at last and tell you to come home with Him."

Then I saw pictures in my mind of Christ dying on the Cross.

"Kemeil, God is showing me He knows how I feel because He had to watch His son, Jesus, die on the Cross. Jesus knows how you feel because in His flesh, He felt like God had forsaken Him. The flesh doesn't like pain. Also, in the Garden of Gethsemane, Christ's flesh wanted the cup to pass. But then the Spirit of God spoke the words 'nevertheless, not my will but thy will be done'. "So Kemeil, whatever God's will be, we are yielding to His will."

After I said these words, Kemeil closed her eyes, bowed her head, and squeezed my hand as she silently prayed to God. "That's right, baby, surrender all to Him," I said.

I always wished I knew what she told God, but whatever she said, God accepted it, because a few days later she passed away.

CHAPTER NINE
The Last Day

The last day I saw Kemeil was on January 9, 2018. I remember slowly walking down the hallway to go to the I.C.U. area when someone came out to meet me. I honestly think I stopped breathing, bracing myself for the worst.

I was told that Kemeil had been moved to a room in the hospital. I rushed to her side. She was in bad shape; Her urine had blood in it. She tried to eat some pureed food, but going down, it made this weird, hollow sound. She was struggling to breathe. Also, one of her eyes slightly drooped.

"She don't look good," the nurses told me.

While I was there, I arranged for Kemeil to go to hospice at a different facility other than Manor Care. She had previously flat out refused to go to hospice, but with much pleading and praying, on that last day I saw her, she consented to go.

I always told her through this whole ordeal that I would never tell her goodbye. Saints of God know (even at death) that they will one day see each other again. Whenever I had to leave her to go back home, I wouldn't tell her goodbye. I would say "I love you," and she would say "Love you" in return. I would kiss her on the forehead, we would look at each other, and I would leave.

I never knew when it would be the last time I would see her. When I went to leave her that day, after saying "I love you" and kissing her on the forehead, we just looked at each other for a few moments longer. I didn't want to upset her by telling her I was going back to New York, so I didn't say anything more. I believe we both had the same thoughts in our minds.

Would this be the last time we would see one another?

I returned home to New York the next day, January 10. That night, I received a call that Kemeil needed to get a blood transfusion. Elder Gillispie and his daughter, Jasmine, went to the hospital to see her because I thought I had left her cell phone in the room. Turns out that I had it with me in New York and didn't know it. But God does all things well. No one was going to visit Kemeil that day. So, it was a blessing from the Lord that Kemeil had saints to see her. Elder Gillispie held her hand while they gave her the transfusion. They would be the last ones to see her alive.

During my phone call with Elder Gillispie, he asked me if I wanted to talk to her. I said no because I didn't want to let her know that I was back in NY. I thought she would get upset if she knew I had left Maryland.

"Is she in any pain?" I asked him. "She said 'no'," he told me.

"Tell her I love her," I said.

To this day, I remember that moment and think I should have talked to her one more time. But God knows best, and Kemeil didn't need me to break down on the phone. At least that's how I comfort myself about that day. The most important thing to me is that she knew I loved her, and that's all that mattered.

The Victory at Last!

On January 11, 2018 at approximately 3:30am, I got that call no parent wants..Kemeil had passed.

Life was never the same for our family from that moment.

The craziest thing I realized about myself was that it shocked me to hear those words: she passed! I really don't think I expected her to die, at least not that soon. Looking back on it now, I know it's sound ridiculous to think that, but at that moment, I had a really hard time processing that Kemeil was really gone!

Even after the funeral, after everyone went back to their normal lives, I still felt like Kemeil was in Pennsylvania. It probably was best that way. If Kemeil had lived with me in New York, I know I would have taken her death a whole lot harder.

After ending the call with the doctor, what Jesus said in John 19:30 came to my mind; "It is finished!" (KJV) Kemeil's journey had completed and my prayers had been answered. God got the glory, and the Devil was defeated! Her soul was returned back to the Lord, and the Devil couldn't trouble her anymore, Hallelujah!

To Sum It All Up

Over her entire life, Kemeil tried to carry childhood hurts and pains into adulthood alone. When she looked to others to take away her daily anguish, she was disappointed in their inability to do so. Although she grew up in the church from age one until her twenties, Kemeil, like so many young people who start off with Jesus but turn away, was persuaded by the enemy of her soul that church didn't have what she needed.

My daughter had sat through years of preaching, bible teaching, and Sunday School, but she never had developed a one-on-one personal relationship with God. Like she stated to us on more than one occasion, "I am thirty- seven years old and never knew God."

So, it is very possible to be in the church *but not be in Christ at the same time.*

The reality of Kemeil's problem was that the only person she could totally place her burdens on was Jesus Christ. We were never made to bear our own burdens. Others can share our grief and pray to God to take the person's pain, *but only God can carry those burdens and give us peace in its place.*

Jesus died on the cross for our sins. So, in other words, Christ took upon Himself the heavy weight of our sin and guilt. Isaiah 53:5-6 says:

But he was wounded for our transgressions, he was bruised for our iniquities: the chastisement of our peace was upon him; and with his striped we are healed. All we like sheep have gone astray; we have turned every one to his own way; and the LORD hath laid on him the iniquity of us all." (KJV)

Everything we need is in Christ. There was a choir song I used to lead that said, "there is no way I can live without God." Living without God is unbearable. Alcohol, drugs, promiscuity, and suicide are not the answers. No man, woman, house, child, job, material wealth, or fame can give you the peace that only comes from God.

In this life, we are going to have problems. There is no escape from problems. It was painful to see Kemeil in physical and mental anguish. When she died, I didn't know how I would go on in her absence. But I did know who I could lean on to carry me through my heartache: Jesus, my Lord and Savior! Psalm 147:3 says "He health the broken in heart, and bindeth up their wounds." (KJV) God did that for Kemeil, and He took her home to be with Him. He did that for me and inspired me to write her story.

Reader, He can do the same for you. No matter what your story, your hurt, or your heartache is, just let Jesus fix it for you!

No, the problem may not go away, but Jesus can take the pain away. Let Jesus fix it for you!

God gave Kemeil a dream in the beginning of this journey with cancer that neither one of us understood. That dream would later reveal itself as true.

In it, Kemeil wore a white bridal dress and stood outside of the Progressive Holiness Church. She knew the groom and the invited guests were waiting for her to come in. However, Kemeil didn't want to go in the church to get married though, in reality, Kemeil very much wanted to get married.

How the dream came to pass was this: Kemeil's funeral was on January 23, 2018. She was funeralized at Progressive Holiness Church in Hempstead, NY. She was dressed in a white suit. As I stated earlier in this book, she didn't want to die. Her groom was Christ Himself. The viewing and funeral had so many attendees, people had to come in shifts. They came from everywhere. Old coworkers, friends, and members of other churches from near and far, and people from other states attended.

Truly, Kemeil got the best homegoing that could ever be asked for. To God be the glory!

CHAPTER TEN
The Book of Whys

Since humans have walked the face of the earth, we have asked the same question.

Why?

I'm no different; I asked God why Kemeil had to die from cancer at thirty- eight-years young. Why didn't He heal her, so she could be a powerful witness to His saving grace and healing powers?

After all, I heard about those whom God had healed of cancer. Why not heal Kemeil?

I don't have answers to my questions in this book nor do I have answers for any of your why questions either. All I can say is that we will always ask God why for every difficult situation, and we may spend a lifetime seeking the answers.

If it were possible to write "The Book of Whys," the volume sets would probably fill an entire room from ceiling to floor, front to back. I, alone, would have several volumes. Our whys are usually directed towards God, and by questioning the Almighty, the undertone hints at blame.

"Why did you allow this God? Why didn't you stop this God? Why won't you answer me, Lord? Why?"

Those who don't believe in God use "why" questions against those who yet believe in God despite calamities. Someone reading this book may ask me,

"Why do you serve a God who allowed these things to happen to your daughter and you?" Add that question to our invisible Book of Whys.

Some would attempt to answer our whys. When someone very sick dies, we say things like "their suffering is over, and they are in a better place." We say this to soothe the pain of the loss. We try to make sense as to why this person was taken away from our lives. Sometimes we say, "God knew best." In other words, we try so hard to come up with our own answers. Not to say that these answers are not true. It's just something I have observed that we do in time of grief.

Have you ever watched a sitcom where a child is sitting at the dinner table refusing to eat his vegetables? The mother comes over and says something like this, "Tommy eat your vegetables; they are good for you."

Then Tommy, who is allowed to express his feelings, asks her "Why?" The mother then says, "So you can grow big and strong like Daddy." Again, Tommy asks "Why?"

The mother may then try to explain scientifically why he should eat his veggies. After several rounds of this "why" challenge, in frustration, the mother finally says, "Because I said so!"

I don't know who invented this phrase but it's excellent at ending a child's never-ending "why" exercises. True story: I personally made the "why" question a curse word in my house.

I believe sometimes God just listens to our questions and doesn't respond. Here are my reasons for believing this:

1. We wouldn't accept His answer if He told us why
2. We would think our way of handling a situation was better than God's way.
3. We wouldn't understand His answer. Read Isaiah 55:8-9.

Have you ever dealt with an angry person who kept questioning you? No matter how hard you tried to explain your answer to them, they refuse to accept it. Sometimes, we are like this with God and refuse to calm down or be wrong in our thinking.

Did you know we are not the only ones who asked God why? The Bible tells of many people who had questions, too. Job is famous for his whys. In Job 1:6, it says "there was a day when the sons of God came to present themselves before the Lord, and Satan came also among them (KJV). Here's the short version of the story:

God: "Where have you been, Satan?" Satan: "Doing what I want to do." God: "Have you tried my servant, Job?"

Satan: "You are protecting him so I can't do anything to him. If you let me at him, he'll curse you."

God: "Granted. Touch his things, but not him."

The entire book of Job is full of whys and when we read his story, we can understand his questions. After all, in one day, Job lost: oxen, donkeys, servants, sheep, camels, and ten children! Oh, and it didn't stop there. God later granted Satan permission to afflict Job's body. This was overwhelming, and here are some of the questions Job asked God:

Job 3:11 "Why died I not from the womb?" (KJV)

Job 4:7 "Remember, I pray thee, whoever perished, being innocent? or where were the righteous cut off?" (KJV)

Job 6:11 "What is my strength, that I should hope? And what is mine end, that I should prolong my life?" (KJV)

Job asked his questions amid great grief and afflictions. Job's friends even asked questions. They accused him of sinning, but Job insisted he did nothing wrong. I want to mention here that God didn't answer any of Job's questions. Not one. In fact, at the end of this story, God asked Job questions:

Job 38:1-4 "Then the Lord answered Job out of the whirlwind, and said, Who is this that darkeneth counsel by words without knowledge? Gird up now thy loins like a man; for I will demand of thee, and answer thou me. Where wast thou when I laid the foundations of the earth? declare, if thou hast understanding." (KJV)

This story ends in victory. Job repents for being self-righteous. God tells him to pray for his friends, who were wrong about him, and God blesses him with ten more children and much more of the amount of cattle he had before. Hence the saying "double for his trouble."

The Bible doesn't tell us what Joseph's questions were, but I imagined he had many. However, many years after his brother sold him into slavery over their jealousy of him, Joseph was able to explain to his brothers, whom he had forgiven, why God allowed terrible things to happen to him.

Genesis 45:5-8: "Now therefore be not grieved, nor angry with yourselves, that ye sold me hither: for God did send me before you to preserve life. For these two years hath the famine been in the land: and yet there are five years, in the which there shall neither be earing nor harvest. And God sent me

before you to preserve you a posterity in the earth, and to save your lives by a great deliverance. So now it was not you that sent me hither, but God: and he hath made me a father to Pharaoh, and lord of all his house, and a ruler throughout all the land of Egypt." (KJV) So, whether God explains to us why He does what He does, or we understand his decisions, God always knows what He's doing. I have my own theories as to why God didn't heal Kemeil, but her funeral was a testament to God's forgiving grace. I will NEVER forget the preacher's message "The Eleventh- Hour Saint." If you want to see the entire funeral, it is available on YouTube as "Kemeil Thompson's funeral."

I don't know if I'll ever completely understand why Kemeil is not with us. It has taken me four years to get the courage to write her story. But, I do know that without Kemeil, there wouldn't be a book. I do know that God got the glory at the end of her life. I do know that, like the hymn by Bill and Gloria Gaither, "because He (Christ) lives, I can face tomorrow."

GONE BUT NOT FORGOTTEN

Poetry from the heart of Kemeil Patrice Thompson

Kemeil had many talents. One of them was writing. When a group of us cleaned out her townhouse, my daughter, Lisa, and son-in-law, Harold, found a couple of books and many pages of writing she had penned. We never knew she had written them until that moment. So, I kept them and selected some to be published in this book. They range from funny to agonizingly serious.

As I read through her poetry, my heart broke all over again. I could see the transition from one stage to another in her life -- words of loneliness, regret, anger, love she desperately tried to find in men who eventually rejected her, and in so many other emotions.

At first, I intended to only include the happy poems but decided that wasn't a realistic picture of who Kemeil was. Some of them are dark and may cause you to shed a tear. But allowing them to be read further proves what I have said throughout this book. Without God's help, we are lost and miserable when we try to handle difficult/impossible things on our own.

I pray you will learn from her pain and take your burdens to the Lord. Only Jesus Christ can give us peace in the times of trouble and take the heavy burdens we try to bear on His mighty shoulders. In this world, we can never escape pain, but we can give it to Jesus, who in turn replaces it with peace, joy, and contentment. Sharing these precious writings with you is my way of remembering that Kemeil is gone but not forgotten, God bless you.

12-16-96

The Night I Understood My Mother

The night I understood my mother
Came quite unexpected
As usual, she had a solution to a situation,
But unlike usual, I accepted it.

The night I understood my mother
Started off quite dreary
But right away her solution made sense,
Perhaps, because her tone was relaxed,
And her approach rather silly.

The night I understood my mother
I was overjoyed with what I'd finally seen.
When closely examined, my mother
Was nothing more than an older picture of me.

So, upon having always understood myself And seeing her now,
I understood my mother.

Thank you, Jesus!!

1-26-97
A Cause To Relax

I used to worry about having "good brains,"
But then I made a couple of "As" and "Bs.".
I used to worry about being athletic,
Until I ran faster than anyone had ever seen.

I used to worry about death,
But then I got saved.
I used to worry about talent,
Until I started writing and drawing…
Still do to this day.

I used to worry about friends.
So, I decided to get them any way I could.
I used to worry about loved-ones,
So, I prayed that all that befell them, was good.

And lastly,
I used to worry about having a dad,
Until I met Jesus and my pastor.
I used to worry about having a best friend,
'Til fortunately I found one.
And am living happily ever after.

Worries come and go.
And solutions glide by every once in a while.
The way each of us handle them,

Patricia Varner

Is what makes us unique and versatile.

Everyone worries,
But I conclude given the facts…
It is much easier on one's health,
If one would just relax.

2-22-97

A Doorkeeper's Prayer

Dear Lord,
Please help me to smile.
To make some visitor's visit
To certainly have been worthwhile.

Dear Lord,
Please help me to be patient.
When some saint's child will not listen,
And the parent does the same,
Help me not to become aggravated.

Dear Lord, Please help my feet.
And when my corns hurt me most,
Help me to remain sweet.

Dear Lord,
Please just help me to be a good doorkeeper.
This is my prayer,
That you continue to guide me.

And keep me under your care
As I stand watch there.

8 - 10 - 97

Forgetting Something?

Somewhere!... Way down a deep, dark alley,
There's a lil' ol' peddler
Who's in need of your hospitality.

Oh-so ya say you don't like alleys?
Brings back too many memories?
Aw, that's too bad... Oh-well, maybe some other time.

But somewhere... Deep down behind a smelly old dumpster,
There's a poor lil' runaway
Who's in need of your hospitality and comfort.

But what's that now?
Ya say you don't go nowhere near garbage?
Been around it all your life?
Oh-well, that's just too bad... Maybe the next passerby will help.

Yet and still, Sometimes... Right in that ol' church you go to.
Oh, I know you only make your grand appearance-
Every once-in-awhile...

But I'm quite sure you have seen this person a time or two.
Was it that ol' wise mother, who was always just-a-prayin'?
Or was it that shoutin' deacon?
Or maybe it was that mean ol' usher
Who told you to keep quiet while that ol' preacher was preachin'?

In the Shadow of My Daughter's Death

Well, whoever it was… Surely you won't mind lending them a hand.
It wouldn't hurt you none to send them some flowers,
Or to plant a few dollars in their suffering hands.

Ah, now I remember who it was… And you should too.
That poor, needy, raggedy person
Wasn't nobody else but you.

Oh how soon we forget,
When it's our turn to help.
It's a shame… The only time we remember
Is when we need the help ourself.

05-2003

A Faithful Relationship

My relationship with You
Means all the world to me.
Each day I spend with You
Strengthens my faith in thee.

Neither death nor life
Fear I
As long as Christ
Walks by my side.

I know You exist
And watch over me each day.
A reality, not a myth,
I believe You to be when I pray.

With joyful praise
Will I live out my days.
For none on earth has proven as true
To their promises as You.

Therefore, I believe in Your love,
Your grace, Your power,
And Your generous mercy
In my most sinful hour.

A just God

In the Shadow of My Daughter's Death

Christ is

And despite that Satan's entices
Me to sin continuously
I strenuously
Try to obey the God within me.

He has saved me from so many things
That I
Have no other choice, but to
Believe in Christ.

05-2003

The Testimony

There once was a woman
Who never ever seemed to frown
And people often inquired
Why she never ever seemed down.

"Do you ever have a bad day?"
They always use to say
And she would always reply
"As long as Christ liveth, how could I?"

Then one day she rose to tell
Her testimony of which none knew well
And those that sat in the mist
Heard the woman say something like this…

"A tale of life in the city,
Of the best and worst times
My brain could ever fathom
Brings forth to my mind."

"A thought ladened with pity
For myself as I lay there
Helplessly drowning in the city
And overwhelmed by despair."

"For you see,

In the Shadow of My Daughter's Death

I needed help

But help was nowhere to be found
And all I could see
Was problems
For miles around."

"Then along came a Savior
Able to do all I could not do
And this is why I can offer
This assurance to you…"

"Faith is the victory
For all who step out in the belief
That Christ will never fail
To deliver them relief,
Aid, or comfort
And whatever else they might ask.
So put your trust in God whose power
None other can surpass."

0 5 - 2 0 0 3

Look Up

When you feel
All is lost
During times when
Unbelievable burdens,
Your patience, exhaust
And trusting and obeying
Are mere sayings
That you hear
While the uplifting hymns of faith
Bypass your ear-
Look up.

When your past haunts your future
And you wish your present was not around
To remind you of the mistakes
That cause you to frown
In addition to the reservoir of tears
You've accumulated over the years
Along with the fears
You've always clung to
Hoping that they never come to
Pass-
Look up.

When all your friends are gone
And your luck has run out

In the Shadow of My Daughter's Death

Adding loneliness

To the already long list
Of things you want out
Of your life this minute
Realize they would be
If God was in it
And- Look up.

Look up to the hills
From whence cometh all help
While trusting that he'll
Take care of you and all else.

Have faith in Christ
And He will do the rest
For as long as your faith
Of Him continually requests.

5-5-04

Grandpa

Part 1

"Life is like a mountain railroad with an engineer that's brave. We must make the run successful from the cradle to the grave…"

That was my grandfather's favorite line of a song that depicted the reason why my life's gone wrong.

Grandpa, I have not been making the run successful, as I have not had control of my extremely stressful life due to my desire to please those around me who aspire to drive me insane with their games, their lies, and their deceit because their own weak excuses for lives have made them miserable and in the literal sense their misery strives to gather as much company as it possibly can, but as I now take control of my own train, I will not stand for this madness anymore.

Within the grave of Grandpa lies the horrid, thorny crown I used to wear along with the cross not born by Christ, but by my miserably lost childhood followed by my later years and all the tears shed as I stood there struggling with my identity, with my mother and my family, but more importantly, myself, thinking how else can I respond to the surge of such a commanding force as my own church and the only family I have known having have forever lived within their home?

My family and I are no longer one, instead two separate entities we have now become causing my view to have been cleared allowing the rays of the sun to shine for the first time on me.

Here I stand all alone determined to make within this world a home of my own, boldly facing my destiny and my fears having dried all my past tears…

Part 2

All I need now is my own strength, all I want now is one sensitive soulmate with which to share all of me and all my affairs, perhaps a child or two will do nicely as long as I choose their father wisely, a home of some sort, a car or two or three, and a great job would complete me.

Now some of this I already have and what I don't I'll continue to go after until I do stand happily in the wind having erased all the past hurt within my heart, soul and brain successful running my own train.

I can only hope to make you proud, grandpa.

R.I.P. 03-29-04

*Kemeil had a close relationship with the man whom she called "Grandpa," but they were not related. This writing apparently was written thirty-seven days *after* he passed. He never got to read this, and I only discovered it when preparing for this book.

He was a man she highly respected and looked up to, especially since she never had a father figure in her life.

I want to mention that at the time of this writing, this was *Kemeil's perception of reality; her truth*. She expresses how she felt. The content shows the mental tumult that raged within her and that she was trying to come up with her own resolution.

Since the writing was directed to only him, it can be concluded that she felt he was the only one she could confine in. But the irony of this reading is that she never intended for him to know her true feelings.

(UNDATED)
Thinking Out Loud

Heartful thoughts
Thinking of finding myself.
Slowly, but surely realizing
I can rely on no one else.

Somedays I like me
And some I wish I were someone else,
But every day I am me
So, I have no choice but to be myself.

I am trying to I
mprove the quality of my life,
But this is not easy
On either my in or my outsides.

My glasses are always dirty
Making it hard for me to see
What path I should take
And what should I keep away from me.

Today should've been a sick day,
But my life would never allow
Me to have my own way
And so I am here now.

I know I look horrible

Patricia Varner

I left my house half-dressed
And the first person I laid eyes on
Is not who I'd want to see me a mess.

When I'm happy
I want to write, but I don't
So, I apologize if all my poems
Seem sad
But please understand that it's hard
For me to praise the few
Good feelings that I've had.

I'm not depressed
Just disappointed
With my life in general
And I often wonder
If this will change anytime
Before my funeral.

I rarely ever
Get what I want
And this is quite frustrating
Especially when
Everyone around me does
Making me crazy.

*This poem was extremely hard for me to read and include in this book. Though it has no date, from what it says I believe Kemeil was going through chemo treatments, her condition was getting worse, and she was close to the end of her life. She mentions "it should have been a sick day." She went to work many times because she didn't want to lose her position as manager. She was being pressured to take a lower position. Many of her poems are written on work stationary.

What helped me to continue to finish this book was knowing Kemeil's mental and physical suffering was OVER, and she is in the presence of God happy at last.

(UNDATED)

The Responsibility

I've been around the world and back
And still have yet to see
MLK's dream become a fact
Bringing peace, love, and equality.
From Haiti to Korea and then Iraq
The blood-stained earth screams in pain
As each day the seas redden just a tad
More than they were before the sixth day came
Life, oh how bittersweet the taste
When you live as one of the human race,
But bear in mind that the main rule of the game is
So handsomely supplied by Darwin's "Survival of the fittest."
And fit we are, America, oh mighty great nation
May we never fall or become God-forsaken.
If we ignore our flaws, it's only because
That we are the best, we are aware of
For it is not the nicest nation that wins
But the strongest because it can endure to the end
So, stand tall as earth's mighty champion, ready to oversee
The responsibility of the oblong empire that has been given to thee

AUTHOR—PATRICIA VARNER

It's Alright

I miss you so much each day, each week
In others your image I sometimes seek
Is that Kemeil there? Is that her face?
I'm reminded of you all over the place

Memories come of your pain and fear
The struggles you had bring me a tear
Then I remember, it's okay
God took your spirit far, far away

Satan can't torment you anymore
Cancer can't follow you pass Heaven's door
You're no longer lonely, no longer stressed
You're nothing but loved, peaceful, and blessed

Each year passes, but not our love
I'm still pressing on 'til I join you above
I'm taking the lessons that I learned with you
Passing them to others, yes I do

Letting all know, God's hand is extended
There is hope; their lives can be mended
Telling your story in your stead
Praying they'll think about what I've said

I go to your gravesite now and then

Patricia Varner

Talking to the dirt, thinking what's been
I know I speak to just a shell
My baby is with God; all is well

The shadow of death has been defeated
No more will your sorrow be repeated
Yes, I'm left to tell your story
It's alright, may God get the glory

Good Times

During Kemeil's life there were many happy moments despite the sadness recorded in this book. These are some of the selected pictures that I love to look at because they remind me of happier days. The following is a visual gallery of those captured times.

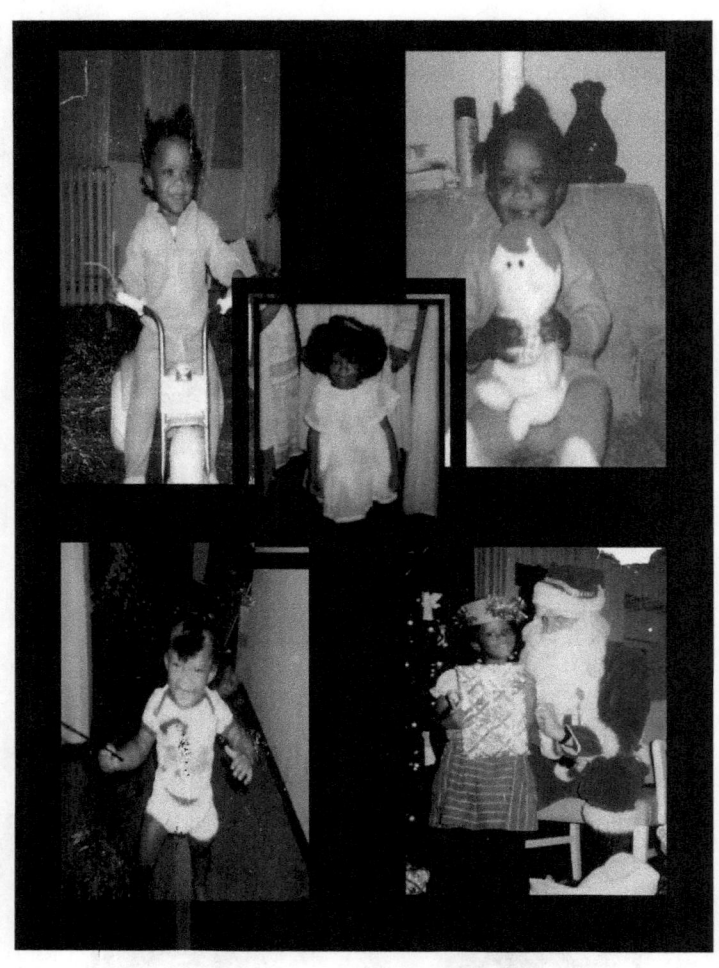

In the Shadow of My Daughter's Death

Kemeil as flower girl for my wedding

Patricia Varner

In the Shadow of My Daughter's Death

In the Shadow of My Daughter's Death

Patricia Varner

www.ingramcontent.com/pod-product-compliance
Lightning Source LLC
Chambersburg PA
CBHW060338050426
42449CB00011B/2786